KINGDOM KREATORS
MOUNTAIN TOP INTERNATIONAL

Guardians

Of

Spiritual

Maturity

Guardians Of Spiritual Maturity

Cover Graphic Designer – Craig Danforth/Natcom1.com
All interior images printed by permission – Pexels.com & Pixabay.com

ISBN 978-0-9815944-1-5

December 2016

Printed in the United States of America
A special thanks to Craig Danforth, Chris Davis, Sheryl Jones and Michael Murphy for your contribution in the editing of this book.

Also, a very special thanks to my wife Tamera for her enormous amount of input and assistance in all I do.

For information regarding
permissions to reproduce
material from this book, please
email or write:

Michael A. Danforth
Mountain Top International
PO Box 43
Yakima, Washington 98907
www.mticenter.com

Table Of Contents

Guardians Of Spiritual Maturity

My hope is everyone who reads this book will be inspired to reach higher; to go further and deeper into the supernatural revelation of the heart of God.

If I were to sum up my intent for writing this book, it is to encourage people to manifest the love of God to the highest degree possible. In addition, it is to occupy heaven for the purpose of revealing that same glory on Earth. In addition, I would like to make you aware of the temporal guardianship currently in place, until, the maturation of the body of Christ. We are the chosen ones;

destined to participate in the restoration of all things, thus do far more than any other generation before us.

"Now to him who is able to do far more abundantly than all that we ask or think, according to the power at work within us." (Ephesians 3:20)

Here is a more extended version of this same verse.

Now, in the One being continuously able and powerful to do, to make, form, create and produce above and beyond all things that we are repeatedly asking for ourselves or are normally grasping with the mind, or, apprehending, imagining, considering or conceiving in accord with the power and ability, which is continuously operating, making itself effective, energizing itself, working and developing within us, and in union with us. In Him is the glory and manifestation, which calls forth praise, within the called-out community or the summoned forth congregation of God, as well as, within Christ Jesus, unto all generations of this age and the ages to come. (Jonathan Mitchell NTC)

This is quite an expanded version of *Ephesians 3:20.* My intent is to show the unlimited possibilities God has placed within all of us. There is literally no end to the projected impact of heaven on Earth. *All things are possible.*

In this age and the ages to come, there is nothing God has every created that is outside of our reach. There are a multitude of guardians on Earth, and in heaven, waiting for us to reach for the stars and beyond, and lay hold of our eternal inheritance now.

A countless number of guardians surround us. I'm not just talking about angels and previous saints of glory (cloud of witnesses) but all of creation and its counterparts serve as temporary guardians, waiting for the sons and daughters of God to assume their position in the kingdom of God.

This preservation is necessary until we, the people of God, exhibit a level of spiritual maturity depicting our inherited life in the kingdom of God.

As our spiritual maturation increases, world decay and all of its governing pieces will be brought into submission to the kingdom of God.

As a young man, I grew up in the world of agriculture, primarily in the field of fruit trees.

As the fruit on the trees matured, we had to go through the orchard and place wooden props under the branches loaded down with the heavy weight of the fruit.

I liken the poles we placed under those branches as a necessary support until the fruit could be harvested. Throughout all of creation there are various props that support the natural world around us. These props will not be removed until; God's people reach their intended maturity in his kingdom. At this time, the people of God will become the governmental support of heaven on Earth.

As you read this book, you might be surprised as to the nature of the innumerable guardians that govern this realm called "Earth" and all of the governmental spheres that encompass it.

Before I go on, I want to emphasize one important factor; the real proof of spiritual maturity is revealed in our ability to love one another.

"By this all men will know that you are my disciples, if you have love for one another." (John 13:35)

The icing on the cake of spiritual maturity is when the world sees the people of God expressing a genuine love toward all humanity, not just those considered to be Christian.

In every moment of our life, one way or another, we are engaging with natural and spiritual governments, which can either limit or aid us in our spiritual journey.

These guardians of creation are purposed to serve as a type of tutor until; we grow up into our eternal nature in the kingdom of heaven.

A simple analogy of a spiritual guardian is likened to a tutor in early biblical times. Then, a tutor was a servant whose duty it was to conduct a youth to and from school. The tutor's primary function was to supervise the youth's general behavior, thus keeping the child within the boundaries of parental expectations.

Unlike western practices, the function of a tutor was not that of a teacher, but as a watchman or guardian. In ancient history, a guardian was employed until a child reached a point of maturity, at which time; the child would no longer need a guardian to watch over him or her.

In this same way, the Law of Moses was a guardian to faith. Once faith appeared on the scene, this ancient guardian was no longer needed for the next stages of spiritual maturity.

In the book of Galatians, Paul describes it like this,

"Before faith came, we were kept in custody under the law, being shut up to the faith which was later to be revealed. Therefore, the Law has become a tutor (guardian) to lead us to Christ, so that we may be justified by faith. Now that faith has come, we are no

longer under a tutor (guardian). For you are all sons of God through faith in Christ Jesus." (Gal 3:23-27)

Here we can see the declination of a previous guardian is an indicator of spiritual maturity. When we entered into our mentorship with Jesus Christ; we came out from under the guardian of the Law, thus an open declaration of our spiritual maturity, beginning at an entirely new level.

The moment we entered into Jesus Christ, we were instantaneously transferred into an awareness of our true creative state in the kingdom of God. However, while the action of entering into Christ is instantaneous, the reality of growing up into the mind of Christ is a progressive work.

"...We are transformed by the renewing of our mind, in order that we may prove what the will of God is, that which is good, acceptable and perfect." (Romans 12:2)

Though we have been brought into Christ we are still learning to walk in the revelation of His mind. In this sense, we are transformed by the renewing of our minds. Through a continual renewing of our mind, the perfection of Christ in us becomes much more apparent.

Growing up into the mind of Christ means growing up into the revelation of His love. In the epicenter of His love is a state of spiritual maturity, which breaks us free from all of the tutorials of life.

Another way of viewing "guardians of spiritual maturity" is seeing the physical world as a temporary state and the invisible world as eternal.

"...while we look not at the things which are seen, but at the things which are not seen; for the things which are

seen are temporal, but the things which are not seen are eternal." (Romans 4:18)

This does not mean that every natural thing will be destroyed, but it does imply all creation in its temporary state, will eventually be swallowed up by the eternal atmosphere of heaven on Earth. The end result is the restoration of all things.

Speaking of Jesus,

"...whom heaven must receive until the period of restoration of all things about which God spoke by the mouth of His holy prophets from ancient time." (Acts 3:21)

Again, the Law, from Old Testament times, was just one of many guardians given to preserve the people of God until their time of spiritual maturation. As you will soon discover, every natural form of government on Earth is at best a temporary guardian, until the manifestation of the sons/daughters of God is realized.

These governments entail every aspect of creation, including all the laws of physics. Whether light, gravity, climates, seasons etc., humanity has become so earthly minded it struggles accessing the kingdom realms of heaven. Through the portal of God's love we have been given full access to all of heaven's eternal counterparts.

Thus, the intended eternal government of heaven on Earth is yet to be fully realized. We are being petitioned by the courts of God to assume our seats in heavenly places, thereby, relieving the guardians of creation from duties of temporal preservation. Since the beginning, when all things were spoken into existence, that same breath has continued to sustain all of creation.

Through Jesus Christ, we have been reinstated/reconciled with the Father. Therefore, even the governmental operations within the church, which include every level of gifting and any other spiritual administration, are destined to surrender their governance to the eventual maturation of heaven on Earth.

Of course, all the above will continue functioning on the Earth until the final appearing of Jesus Christ. When Jesus walked upon the Earth, he modeled the power of sonship and what it was like to override every spiritual and natural force of creation. Regardless of natural or spiritual forces, Jesus executed his kingdom authority over all.

Jesus wasn't limited to any field of gifting. Whatever he saw the Father doing was what he did. **Jesus wasn't "gifted" minded, he was sonship minded.**

All the gifts and callings of God are an expression of God's love. The moment Jesus, the Word, became flesh and dwelt among us, the entire human race became subject to a glory, to a love so full of grace and truth it defied every spiritual and physiological law known to man.

Every natural and spiritual force was subject to the authority of Jesus. Jesus demonstrated his authority over the winds and seas, from walking on water, multiplying loaves and fishes, raising the dead, to casting out demonic forces; all were just a brief preview into his endless ability to bring everything into alignment with the kingdom of his Father.

As already mentioned, there are various laws at work in the natural and in the spirit, which are subject to change at any moment. The eventual transformation of all things is waiting for the supernatural genius of heaven in you, to alter their state from a lesser to a greater function of kingdom glory.

Right now, the beginning stages of these divine transformations are occurring in ways most never dreamed possible. Thus, awakening the people of God into the destined expectations of the endless love of heaven, here now.

We carry the supernatural DNA of a Father whose primary purpose is to bring us into the realization of who we are in Him and Him in us, thus experiencing an amazing love that reaches into endless fields of possibilities.

The Storehouses Of Heaven

In the morning of July 24, 2014, I was awakened at 4:00AM hearing these words;

"A large gate made up of men and women of God who have been accessing heaven, is opening up wide; wider than any other period since the beginning of Christianity."

Of course, I immediately thought of David,

"Lift up your heads, O gates,
And be lifted up, O ancient (everlasting) doors,
That the King of glory may come in! (Ps 24:7)

"Lifting up your heads" is in reference to heavenly authority. It is the government of heaven coming through the people of God. In this sense, the head represents the action of the heart, **"as a man thinks in his heart."** We think and see from the heart, not the head.

The head is the storage place or hard drive of the heart, which is where the information of the heart is stored. Whenever we set our hearts and minds on things above, we are then lifted up through ancient, everlasting doors, which enable the "King Of Glory" to come through the portals of our being.

Without rehashing some former teachings, I want to cut to the chase and speak about the storehouses of heaven and how our ability to access them enables us to become gates of heaven on earth. Currently, there are many storehouses in heaven, which are being guarded by angels, waiting for the saints of God to gain access to them, thus assuming their authority in heaven.

At the beginning of January 12, 2014, I spoke to the people at MTI on how I gained access to the storehouses of snow as described in the book of Job.

"Have you entered the storehouses of the snow?
Or have you seen the storehouses of the hail,
Which I have reserved for the time of distress,
for the day of war and battle?" (Job 38:22)

This wasn't just some off the wall, by chance experience. This was an intentional effort to access the storehouses of heaven, in this case, the storehouses of snow. After my first experience with the storehouse of snow, the next day, which was Sunday, I invited everyone at our MTI gathering to join me in accessing the storehouse of heaven.

The very next day, the result was a miraculous manifestation of unpredicted snowfall. Mind you, this occurred on the heels of a reported drought in the PNW.

By the end of January and mid-February, the entire Northwest, including Washington, Oregon, Idaho and Montana received all of its winter snow pack.

"Pacific Northwest getting socked with second snow blast" (USA Today, Feb 7, 2014)

"Winter really came in with a vengeance by late January and February. During late January through February time frame the Northwestern pattern became most pronounced, resulting in record snowfall in such a short period of time. (Weather.com)

As you can imagine, this revelation set me on a course to learn more about all the storehouses in heaven and how to gain access to each one. We were seemingly in a moment of entering into an intense drought, yet through faith, we gained access to an endless supply of snow.

Many of you are familiar with the life of Joseph and how God placed him in a position of authority over all the storehouses in Pharaoh's empire.

"So when all the land of Egypt was famished, the people cried out to Pharaoh for bread; and Pharaoh said to all the Egyptians, "Go to Joseph; whatever he says to you, you shall do." When the famine was spread over all the face of the earth, then Joseph opened all the storehouses, and sold to the Egyptians; and the famine was severe in the land of Egypt. The people of all the earth came to Egypt to buy grain from Joseph, because the famine was severe in all the earth." (Genesis 41:55-57)

Joseph was the guardian over all the storehouses, thereby opening them up to all who were hungry. His position of authority turned a season of severe famine into a season of sufficient supply for all

16

those in need.

Not too long after, around July 16, 2014, I felt a strong disturbance in my spirit concerning the forecast of destruction the fire season was presenting in the Pacific Northwest. The intensity of heat and dryness seemed to only give aid to the already out of control burning flames.

During that time, I thought, "there has to be some storehouses in heaven we can be accessing for a time such as this. Mind you, I understand, on the surface, things like this as tragic as they may be, appear to be a part of the natural flow of unwanted acts of nature. Nonetheless, natural or not, I felt a prompting in my spirit to engage with Father concerning the destructiveness of these fires. During that time, I came across this storehouse revelation:

"The Lord will open for you His good storehouse, the heavens, to give rain to your land in its season and to bless all the work of your hand..." (Deuteronomy 28:12)
Yes, there it was, the key I was looking for. This passage of scripture became a gateway for me to gain access to the storehouse of rain.

You see, in heaven there is a "good storehouse" within it is multiple storehouses. Its much like Jesus saying, ***"In my Father's house are many mansions."*** In the house of God there are many levels of glory." In the storehouse of God, there are storehouses of rain designated to give rain to the land in its season.
 I'm not going to get into the facets now, but within the temple Solomon built in his day, there were many storehouses, which contained many things for the house of Lord, including the dedicated things for certain sacraments etc. *(1Cronicles 28:10-12)*
This natural temple is another type and shadow of the storehouses

of God in heaven. All of which are available to us and are being guarded until, we learn how to access them and assume our positions as the legal inherited guardians of God.

In **Deuteronomy 28:11-13**, we read,

"The Lord will make you abound in prosperity, in the offspring (fruit) of your body (womb) and in the offspring of your beast and in the produce (fruit) of your ground, in the land which the Lord swore to your fathers to give you. The Lord will open for you His good storehouse, the heavens, to give rain to your land in its season and to bless all the work of your hand; and you shall lend to many nations, but you shall not borrow. The Lord will make you the head and not the tail, and you only will be above, and you will not be underneath, if you listen to the commandments of the Lord your God, which I charge you today, to observe (to keep and do) them carefully..."

Again we read,

"Then David gave to his son Solomon the plan of the porch of the temple, its buildings, its storehouses, its upper rooms, its inner rooms and the room for the mercy seat; and the plan of all that he had in mind, (in his spirit) for the courts of the house of the Lord, and for all the surrounding rooms, for the storehouses of the house of God and for the storehouses of the dedicated things..." (1Chronicles 28:10-11)

There are many more scriptural references throughout the Bible, which reveal the unique storehouses of heaven, which are available to us today.

There are guardian angles watching over these storehouses. They are watching over them, knowing one-day, the sons and daughters of God, like Joseph, will become the kingdom distributors of heaven on Earth.

The Wardrobe Of Heaven

Prior to my first wife, Lori, fully graduating to heaven, I was seeking the Lord on her behalf, hoping to lay hold of a miracle for her life. She was in constant pain and I could see it was beginning to wear down her will to live.

One morning, while in prayer, I was caught up into what I have come to know as the wardrobe of heaven. The wardrobe of heaven is pretty much like it sounds. It's an eternal fitting room with endless robes designed for various functions in life.

This royal room is where one garment is exchanged for another. It's also a place where one garment is joined to another, as if woven together for multiple functions in life.

The kingdom garment you wear is what defines who you are. The Hebrew meaning for "wardrobe" means to spread out, as if in the spreading out a garment to cover, to display or to adorn.

Ultimately, we are clothed or adorned in the righteousness of God. Every other garment is an addition to this eternal robe of love, which has been afforded to us through the blood of Jesus Christ. Before I finish telling you about my first experience with the wardrobe of heaven, let me first give you some scriptural references behind my heavenly encounter.

Isaiah declared,

"I will rejoice greatly in the LORD, My soul will exult in my God; For He has clothed me with garments of salvation, He has wrapped me with a robe of righteousness, As a bridegroom decks himself with a garland, And as a bride adorns herself with her jewels." (Isaiah 61:10)

In Old Testament times, the robes the priests wore had the power to transmit holiness to anyone who touched them.

"When they go out into the outer court, into the outer court to the people, they shall put off their garments in which they have been ministering and lay them in the holy chambers; then they shall put on other garments so that they will not transmit holiness to the people with their garments." (Ezekiel 44:19)

While these next passages of scripture have been used by others to highlight Joshua's kingdom of heaven encounter with God and satan, I would like to present this same experience primarily within the context of Joshua engaging with the wardrobe of heaven.

"Then he showed me Joshua the high priest standing before the angel of the Lord, and Satan standing at his right hand to accuse him. The Lord said to Satan, "The

Lord rebuke you, Satan! Indeed, the Lord who has chosen Jerusalem rebukes you! Is this not a brand plucked from the fire?" Now Joshua was clothed with filthy garments and standing before the angel. He spoke and said to those who were standing before him, saying, "Remove the filthy garments from him." Again he said to him, "See, I have taken your iniquity away from you and will clothe you with festal robes." (Zechariah 3:1-4)

Zechariah continues,

"Then I said, "Let them put a clean turban on his head." So they put a clean turban on his head and clothed him with garments, while the angel of the Lord was standing by. And the angel of the Lord admonished Joshua, saying, "Thus says the Lord of hosts, 'If you will walk in My ways and if you will perform My service, then you will also govern My house and also have charge of My courts, and I will grant you free access among these who are standing here. (Zechariah 3:5-6)

While standing before the Lord, and his accuser, the filthy garments of Joshua (works of the flesh) were removed, and the robe of righteousness (Jesus Christ) was placed upon him. These robes were described as a "festal robes." This exchange of robes was much like when the prodigal, after squandering his inheritance, returned home to his father's house. Upon his return, the father said,

"Bring quickly the festive robe of honor and put it on him; and give him a ring for his hand and sandals for his feet." (Luke 15:22)

As you can see, this robe was a robe of righteousness, at least in the sense; the father removed the filth from his son by covering him with a robe of honor. It is a picture of a prodigal son being reunited with his royal inheritance, thus the ring and sandals.

In this same sense, the garment of filth is removed from Joshua. In the midst of witnesses, the Father robes Joshua with honor, crowns him with authority, thus declaring his sonship in the kingdom of God.

Now fast forward into New Covenant relationship. Through the blood of Jesus Christ, we have been clothed with robes righteousness and crowned with glory. Therefore, like Joshua, we have direct access to the heavenly realms of God.

Through Jesus, we are afforded the opportunity to govern the house of God and take charge of His courts, some of which, are presently under temporary guardianship. In addition, we have full access (the price was paid through the blood) to all the celestial beings that surrounded Joshua in his hour of inauguration.

The angel of the Lord said, *"I will grant you free access among these who are standing here." (Zechariah 3:6)*

Right now, we have access to all that is necessary to fulfill the divine purpose of heaven on Earth. The wardrobe of heaven is a realm in the kingdom of God that bears any and every garment you would ever need to carry out the will of God for your life. The experience I'm about to share with you is a realm in the kingdom of heaven everyone has access to.

Now, let me go back to my wardrobe encounter with Lori.
As I stated at the beginning of the chapter, Lori was wrestling with an intense physical issue in her life. During that time, I was leaning into the heart of God, hoping to lay hold of a miracle.

One day while in prayer, in the spirit, I found myself standing before a large platform. At the side of the platform was a very large and colorful angel. On either side of the angel, were endless rows of garments as far as the eye could see. Over the top of each wardrobe where the garments were hanging were descriptions of each garment.

There were garments for anything and everything you could imagine. Under each major title, there were multiple subtitles for that particular category. For example, there were countless titles listed under the heading of businesses, arts, sports, medical, education, gifts, etc....

During this encounter, one particular garment caught my eye. It was a deep beautiful red color, outlined with a golden raised pattern. As soon as my attention was fixed on that particular robe, it appeared directly across from the platform where I was standing.

Without hesitation, I said, "That is the garment Lori needs." As soon as those words left my mouth, an angel stood beside the platform with the garment in hand.

Instantaneously, Lori was standing on the platform in front of me. This same angel immediately approached her and removed an old tattered looking garment from her shoulders. He then placed the beautiful robe upon her shoulders. When he did, I could see raised markings going every which way across the back of the robe. I then heard the angel declare, "By His stripes you have been healed."

After this experience, as you can imagine, I was very excited for Lori. I immediately shared my experience with her. As an act of faith, I reenacted my experience with her, placing the robe of healing on her. Remarkably, when Lori awoke the next day, it was though a spirit of death had been lifted off of her. She later shared how she had been wrestling with a spirit of suicide. We rejoiced in her victory. As you can imagine, I was completely surprised by her sudden graduation a few months later.

Nonetheless, I have never doubted my experience with the wardrobe of heaven and the initial impact it had on Lori's life. Obviously, I still have some unanswered questions. In the meantime, I am afforded the wonderful opportunity to engage with this heavenly realm as often as the Lord allows.

The woman in Jesus' day, who had the issue of blood, touched the hem of his garment, believing if she did, she would be healed. I believe she had the revelation of the power of the garment of the Priest of God, as result, the virtue of Jesus flowed into her body and set her free. *(Luke 8:43-48)*

"I will rejoice greatly in the Lord, My soul will exalt in my God; For He has clothed me with garments of salvation, He has wrapped me with a robe of righteousness, As a bridegroom decks himself with a garland, And as a bride adorns herself with her jewels." (Isaiah 61:10)

"Your lips, my bride, drip honey; Honey and milk are under your tongue, and the fragrance of your garments is like the fragrance of Lebanon. (Song of Solomon 4:11)
"Speaking of Zion, awake, awake, clothe yourself in your strength, O Zion; clothe yourself in your beautiful garments, O Jerusalem, the holy city; For the uncircumcised and the unclean Will no longer come into you." (Isaiah 52:1)

Guardians of Fire

"And of the angels He says, "who makes His angels wind, and His ministers a flame of fire." (Hebrews 1:7)

In the summer of 2011, I had an unusual encounter with the fire of God. In attempt to get rid of some unwanted stuff around the house, I was preparing to have a garage sale. During our preparations; walking with an armload of stuff, I tripped over the front porch step and collided with the concrete. In a desperate attempt to break my fall, I threw my arms out in front of me. When I did, I hit the concrete with such force; I broke my wrist in multiple places.

At first, I was reluctant to go to the hospital, but the pain left me no choice. I ended up going to the same hospital where my daughter, Amber, served as an ER nurse. After taking a few x-rays, they called in a specialist who verified the fractures in my rest. They put my arm in a temporary cast, until I could get in to see an orthopedic specialist to determine the best course of treatment.

The injury took place on a weekend; therefore I was unable to see an orthopedic specialist before the coming week.

On the day of my appointment, which was scheduled for the afternoon, I decided to spend some time in morning- prayer.

While I was praying, in my mind, I could see what looked like an old adobe oven. For whatever reason, I had a strong impulse to put my hand into the fire. I repeatedly reached my hand in and out of this unusual fiery blaze. Surprisingly, these burning flames were not hot.

As I continued to hold my hand in the fire, I suddenly found myself standing on a stone pathway; positioned between two high walls of fire.

Without hesitation, like a bird, I spread out my arms into the burning flames, all the while walking down this ancient pathway. Again, to my surprise, like the previous fire before, the flaming walls of fire were not hot. Yet, It was though the fire was burning right through me. I knew these fiery flames were the healing fire of God.

It reminded me of the burning bush in the day of Moses. The voice of the Lord, which came from the fire, did not consume the bush.

"The angel of the Lord appeared to him in a blazing fire from the midst of [b]a bush; and he looked, and behold, the bush was burning with fire, yet the bush was not consumed. So Moses said, "I must turn aside now and see this marvelous sight, why the bush is not burned up." When the Lord saw that he turned aside to look, God called to him from the midst of the bush and said, "Moses, Moses!" And he said, "Here I am." (Exodus 3:2-4)

Through this experience, I learned the frequency of fire in heaven does not burn the same on earth. In heaven, the fire of God is spirit. On Earth, fire is the result of hydrogen bonding with oxygen; it produces water vapor even as the wood burns. Fires burn only when all that atomic shuffling releases enough energy to keep the oxidation going in a sustained chain reaction.

In heaven, none of these physical reactions are present. Therefore, the fire of God is the result of the spirit of God manifesting at a supernatural frequency, which is not subject to the laws of physics. That is the shorter version of much deeper spiritual reality.

Now, Back to my initial experience.

Becoming aware of the time, I realized I was running late for my appointment. After arriving to the doctor's office, they took me to the x-ray room to take a few images before seeing the doctor.

Before long, I was taken to where the doctor was viewing the new x-rays. "Hmmm…this is interesting, these x-rays are showing something much different than the previous ones," he said. "Really?" I replied. "Yes, the earlier images show two hair line fractures, but these only show a faint shadow of where they use to be."

It was then when I knew my experience with the fire of God had taken me to a whole new level.

After contending with the doctor a little while longer for a recorded miracle, I walked away knowing I had a divine encounter with the fire of God.

As I mentioned earlier, I believe 2016 was prophetically marked as the year of extraordinary increasing light. Not too long ago, my wife Tamera made me aware that the same Hebrew word "ore" used for light is also the same Hebrew word for fire; and it's number is 217, or 2017.

Just as there are guardians of light, so there are guardians of fire. These same eternal guardians are waiting for the sons and daughters of God to access the flaming realms of Glory, manifesting the fire of God upon the Earth, thus revealing their spiritual maturation in the kingdom of God.

2017 will be a propelling season, in which, the people of God, will see the fire of God consume some of the darkest and destructive works of the enemy. This future consummation will move across the Earth as a wind of fire unlike any other generation as ever seen before. This coming season of spiritual consummation will manifest, in both, natural and spiritual fields of government.

"Know therefore today that it is the LORD your God who is crossing over before you as a consuming fire. He will destroy them and He will subdue them before you, so that you may drive them out and destroy them quickly, just as the LORD has spoken to you." (Deut. 9:3)

The psalmist David declares,

"The fire goes before Him and burns up His adversaries round about..."(Psalms 97:3)

Today, the very fire that once burned before those in ancient times; destroying all the works of enemy, now burns in us. We are the eternal flames of heaven on Earth. The fire burning in us is an everlasting fire of love, which is destined to devour all the works of the enemy.

God awaits those who have been given access to the fire realms of heaven. Just as I was afforded the opportunity to experience these eternal healing flames of God, so you are invited to do the same. By faith, you are able to step into the revelation of this same fire that supernaturally infused my bones together.

He makes the winds His messengers, Flaming fire His ministers. (Psalms 104:4)

Guardians Of Immortality

Prior to the introduction of sin, humanity was not in submission to Earth as they are today. Working by the sweat of our brow in order to get things to produce is part of a relapse in the former intent of God for humanity.

*"...**Cursed is the ground because of you; through painful toil you will eat food from it all the days of your life. It will produce thorns and thistles for you, and you will eat the plants of the field. By the sweat of your face you will eat bread, til you return to the ground, because from it you were taken; for you are dust, and to dust you shall return." (Gen 3:17-19)***

A large part of the Christian population believes we are still under the curse of sin and death. Most read these scriptures from the perspective of imminent decay. Thus, *"you are dust, and to dust you shall return."* Evidently they didn't get the memo, we are no longer under the curse, hence a new creation in Christ. Which means, we are no longer born of the flesh, (dust) but of the spirit.

"However, you are not in the flesh but in the Spirit, if indeed the Spirit of God dwells in you. But if anyone does not have the Spirit of Christ, he does not belong to Him." (Romans 8:9)

While I believe in the intended purpose of God for our lives, I do not view my time on Earth as merely a brief moment to fulfill destiny before I die. I see heaven in me as an extension of my eternal purpose on Earth, which affords me the opportunity to expand the kingdom of God as in heaven.

We have the opportunity to express the love of God to the greatest extent possible, all the while overcoming every obstacle of the enemy, including the spirit of decay. I believe everyone in the kingdom of God, at one level or another, are destined to remove every obstacle that is standing in their way, which keeps them from walking in the fullness of his love.

I view *"time" as a type of spiritual guardian;* affording us the privilege of growing up into the heart and mind of God to the fullest degree possible in this realm. In retrospect, time is also working against us, rather than for us. Yet, all the while our maturation continues on at a higher level. We are progressing from glory to glory to glory. All hindrances to spiritual maturity on Earth are destined to come under our feet.

At the beginning of 2000, the Lord showed me a generation that would be defined as an **"Incorruptible Generation,"** which is a generation that would not see death. He said, "They will be viewed as the **"Immortal Ones."** So here we are today, living in a generation that will begin to exhibit the ability to live outside of the power of death and decay. Yes, I know, this sounds like another absurd perspective of the future. Nonetheless, physical decay was never meant to be a part of the original design of mankind.

This was the amazing thing about the nation of Israel, when they were delivered out of the hands of Pharaoh. While crossing the desert toward the promise land, their garments did not decay.

"Your clothing did not wear out on you, nor did your foot swell these forty years. (Deut. 8:4)

"I have led you forty years in the wilderness; your clothes have not worn out on you, and your sandal has not worn out on your foot. (Deut. 29:5)

Many Hebraic theologians teach that the garments never decayed; their garments supernaturally grew with the increasing growth and stature of each individual. Their feet were not physically impaired by the years of journey. In addition, those who were destined to enter into the promise land, their physical bodies were supernaturally preserved as well.

Even after sin entered into the world, history shows that mankind lived to be hundreds of years old. Decay was not an instant manifestation. Death and decay developed over hundreds, even thousands of years.

While the decay of humanity was the result of sin and death entering into the world, through the blood of Jesus Christ we were set free from the law of sin and death. Therefore, we have been positioned in Christ to overcome the government of decay.

Being born again is the supernatural act of being set free from a darkened state. One of the major fruits of darkness is physical decay and all of its declining counter parts, which include every form of sickness and disease.

Being cleansed of our sins includes being set free of every physical corruption. The process of physical decay is the result of a government that is contrary to the will and desire of God for his people. When Jesus declared, *"You are the light of the world"* he was highlighting a supernatural restorative process, purposed to restore us back to our intended glory in the kingdom of God.

"Therefore, if any man is in Christ he is a new creature; the old things passed away, behold new things have come." (2Corinthians 5:17)

Many have minimized this passage of scripture into meaning the unwanted "stuff" from our past life has passed away and now we have a new beginning in Jesus Christ. While all that is true, it is equally true we have been set free from the laws of physical corruption, thus physical decay.

While most are still waiting to obtain a glorified body in the afterlife of heaven, countless others are recognizing "***old things have passed away and all things have already come.***" *(2Cor 5:17)* The "new" things are in reference to our present inheritance in the kingdom of God, which affords us the ability to restore all things to their glorious heavenly state.

Only God knows when the last glorious finale of full restoration will come into view. The physical world around us is indeed coming to an end, however, not in the manner many have believed. The end of the world system will come through the supernatural overlay of heaven on Earth. At which time, death and the grave (decay) will be removed and will be no more.

*"...**then shall come to pass the saying that is written: "Death is swallowed up in victory." "O death, where is your victory? O death, where is your sting?" (1Cor 15:54-55)***

Again, the majority of Christian believers view these passages of scripture from the perspective of "when I die I will go to heaven" thus my mortality will be swallowed up by immortality.

While it is true our life continues in another realm called heaven, it is equally true through the resurrection of Jesus; death has already been swallowed up. The victory and sting of death was removed through the resurrection power of Jesus.

Since eternity is in our hearts now, we are privileged to place the spirit of decay beneath our feet. Just because people are still growing old, passing from this realm to the next, does not mean Jesus has not already afforded us the opportunity to take on immortality now. If the sting of death came through sin and the power of sin from the law, then when Jesus died and resurrected we were set free from death, sin and the law, which was the instigator of decay.

Many are disturbed by the possibility of living an endless life here and now, and throughout eternity. Thus, not having to depart from this world through sickness, disease or some other form of decay. To the degree our mind becomes renewed by the spirit of God is the degree our physical body will follow suit. In this sense, we are literally transformed by the renewing of our mind.

The "end of all things" is actually the eventual end of the government sin and death.

I see the end of all things, not as the destruction of all things, but the end of decay. Therefore, we are advancing into the revelation of our eternal state in the kingdom of heaven now.

We are already seated in heavenly places; we are just waiting for our physical bodies to catch up, or more clearly, to be further clothed with the revelation of its heavenly state in Christ. (Eph. 2:6, 2Cor. 5:2-4)

Let me say it again, "decay" is the deterioration of all things," which was the result of the nature of sin coming through the gateway of humanity, subjecting all humanity to the law of time, therefore, the law of eventual death.

On one hand time is an enemy of humanity. On the other hand it is a guardian to spiritual maturity. Time is affording you and me the opportunity to grow up into our destined sonship in the kingdom of God, to such degree; we continually override the power of decay with the power of God's eternal love.

Why does the medical world see death as a disease and yet the majority of the Christian world does not? Science has proven the aging process is an unnecessary deterioration of the physical body.

In addition, scientists are aggressively approaching this disease as they would any other. Much of the medical world is beginning to view death as a disease that can be potentially cured, or at the very least, greatly slowed down.

As men and women of God, we hold the antidote of immortality in our hearts, in our DNA, in the blood of Jesus Christ.

We carry within us the eternal signature of eternal life, which has the power to override death now, not some day in the future.

I realize some of these writings can be a bit challenging, especially if you are someone who has long believed dying a physical death is the only pathway to eternal life, thus a new body that will not decay.

Yet, the truth still remains, through Jesus we already died the necessary death required to put us on the road to immortality. The power of eternity is working in us now. Therefore, daily, we are being swallowed by immortality.

The question to be asked is, "When did this perishable put on the imperishable and this mortal put on immortality?

The word "perishable" is in reference to corruption or destruction. Immortality is translated as *"a condition that is free from both death and decay."*

No matter what form of Greek translations you use to define these words, they will undoubtedly bring you to the same conclusion.

Through the power of Jesus Christ, death and the grave have already been swallowed up. Through his death and resurrection we were set free from the sentence of death, which delivered us from the spirit of corruption and destruction. Consequently, these mortal bodies have *now* been set free from both the power of death and decay.

Right now, God is looking for the power of agreement in order for immortality to manifest upon the Earth. At which time, the revelatory finality of death coming under our feet will be realized.

Agreement is a powerful force in the kingdom of God. The glory and power of God's love was manifested through Jesus Christ. This same love was established through the power of agreement. Prior to going to the cross, Jesus prayed to his Father, *"...not my will be done, but your will be done..." (Luke 22:42)*

Again Jesus declares,

"For I have come down from heaven, not to do My own will, but the will of Him who sent Me." (John 6:38)

As we meditate on these few passages of scripture, (there are plenty more) they are an invitation to come into agreement, knowing, *"all things are possible to them who believe."*

The power of heavenly agreement is building across the Earth; we are aligning ourselves in agreement with those who have gone before us. The body of Christ is increasingly coming into agreement with "no decay." Thus, visible signs of an *"Enoch Generation"* are becoming more apparent every day.

"For where two or three have gathered together in My name, I am there in their midst." (Matthew 18:20)

If God is in the midst of two or three, how much more is God in the midst of 100's and 1000's of people whom are daily coming into agreement with his immortal love covering the Earth.

This glorious agreement becomes prime territory to see the miraculous love of God manifest in unprecedented ways. Right now, we are being offered the opportunity to come into agreement: stepping out of the laws of physics that have far too long governed the natural body. This lingering physical body has been serving as a temporary guardian to spiritual maturity, until we grow up into the knowledge of our true immortal state in the kingdom of God.

"And Jesus went throughout all the cities and villages, teaching in their synagogues and proclaiming the gospel of the kingdom and healing every disease and every affliction." (Matthew 9:35)

"Surely he has borne our griefs and carried our sorrows; yet we esteemed him stricken, smitten by God, and afflicted. But he was wounded for our transgressions; he was crushed for our iniquities; upon him was the chastisement that brought us peace, and with his stripes we are healed." (Isaiah 53:4-5)

It seems very appropriate to end this thought with this conclusive revelation; through the blood of Jesus, we were healed of every sickness and disease, including death and decay. Death is a disease. Your agreement with this kingdom revelation will spark an increasing manifestation of signs and wonders unlike any other generation before us. Come on God!

Guardians Of Light

In these next few chapters, I will be using the words "light and time" somewhat repetitively. Even then, I will have barely scratched the surface of their full meaning and intent.

There is an endless amount of insight concerning the light of God. Prior to sin entering into the equation, light functioned much differently than it does today. What does light look like beyond its natural state?

Many have wondered, "What was "light" prior to the Law of sin and death?

The Hebrew word *"light"* is "ore" which means illumination or luminary. Its root meaning is to 'be luminous. From an eternal perspective, light is not just something that shines on us from the outside in, but it's also shines from the inside out.

When God breathed into us, he breathed spirit and light into us. He breathed his heart and mind into us.

As stated earlier, the Hebrew word for light is "ore" its number is 216, which can be translated to mean 2016. This means 2016 was destined to break a barrier of light, thus mark the beginning of an increasing light age. This was my prophetic word in 2015 for 2016.

Prior to 2016, I prophetically spoke about a shift in the government of the United States, which would reflect a level of light unlike this nation has ever seen before. In addition, I prophetically spoke about the redefining of light and how light technology would go off the charts of previous understanding. So here we are now, at the end of 2016, which has undoubtedly been an historical year of light.

Major gateways concerning the science of light, have opened up, revealing insights into the nature of light, greater than anything we have ever seen. (Brief examples to come later in book)

"Then God said, "Let there be light"; and there was light." (Genesis 1:3)

From God's perspective, the light in him shone forth openly manifesting his eternal glory. The purpose of light was to illuminate the knowledge of God's love through all of creation. This means, the light of God is more visible today than any other time in history.

"For since the creation of the world His invisible attributes, His eternal power and divine nature, have been clearly seen, being understood through what has been made, so that they are without excuse. (Romans 1:20)

Since the creation of the world, his invisible attributes have increasingly come into view. Prior to creation, the attributes of God were confined to an alternate realm. According to this passage of scripture, in light of God's eternal power and divine nature, all humanity is without excuse.

In terms of the spectrums of light, in the kingdom of heaven, the number is infinite. In the natural, we can only see 10-15 spectrums of visible light. As we continue our journey toward spiritual maturity our light capacity will increase. We are repeatedly breaking the barrier of light and will soon emanate and engage with the eternal spectrums of heaven in ways many never thought possible. In the natural, we will begin to see spectrums of light that are currently beyond our field of sight.

In the near future, on a much larger scale, the shining ones will become increasingly visible. In the meantime, light technology will exponentially accelerate off the known grid of discovery. All of which, are the result of the increasing revelation of the light of God.

As light continues to infiltrate all creation, countless galaxies will began to change form and eventually reveal levels of glory unlike anything we have ever seen.

In the early 2000's I saw the Milky Way, hidden planets, and other glorious forms in the cosmos, taking on a splendor that exceeded most anyone's wildest imagination. I literally saw all of creation on the brink of a major glorious light shift.

For the most part, the light of creation is in a darkened state. Its present state is temporal; it mostly serves as a temporary guardian for creation. Many glorious splendors were spoken into existence at the beginning of time; declaring to the world, God is the glorious Creator. However, these creative forms of glory are mere introductions to a more vivid eternal glory, destined to exceed its previous glorious state.

Again, everything that pertains to light is changing. The visibilities of all things are going through a type of supernatural metamorphous. Just as the law was a guardian to faith, so are the natural lights serving as a temporary guardian, until, the maturation of the sons/daughters of God.

In the final stages of eternal illumination, there will be no need for the sun and moon. The light in us will ultimately become the light of the world.

When Jesus was transformed into light, he opened up a portal in the spirit, illuminating Moses and Elijah, who were part of an alternate spiritual realm.

There's a glorious army of sonship appearing on the Earth in this present hour and it's getting brighter and brighter every day. Joel describes how the universe will respond to the revelation of these eternal lights:

"The Earth quakes before them, the heavens tremble; the sun and moon grow dark, and the stars diminish their brightness." (Joel 2:10)

This supernatural illumination is making way for a greater glory and perception of God's kingdom. Now, the sun and moon are moving into a bowing position, ready to give up their light to the King of all lights.

The guardians of light are preparing for the light of heaven to make its grand entrance. They are cheering our ability to see beyond the temporal realm, into the eternal.

"While we look not at the things which are seen, but at the things which are not seen; for the things which are seen are temporal, but the things which are not seen are eternal." (2 Cor. 4:18)

Countless people are still waiting for the light of the world to come again. Yet, prior to the departure of Jesus, he made one thing very clear,

"You are the light of the world, a city set on a hill cannot be hidden. (Matt 5:4)

We are evolving into the city of God, one that cannot be hidden. John saw the new eternal city coming out of the heavens, no longer needing the light of the sun or moon.

"But I saw no temple in it, for the Lord God Almighty and the Lamb are its temple. The city had no need of the sun or of the moon to shine in it, for the glory of God illuminated it. The Lamb is its light. And the nations of those who are saved shall walk in it's light, and the kings of the Earth bring their glory and honor into it. Its gates shall not be shut at all by day (there shall be no night there.)" (Rev 21:22-26)

As we go up, all that is in heaven comes down. We are part of this amazing city of God that has no need for the sun or moon to shine in. The light of God is already shining in and through us. Therefore, we will walk in the light as He is in the light. The gates, which we are, will never be shut again. Never again, will darkness penetrate our hearts.

"Lift up your heads, O gates, and lift them up, O ancient doors, that the King of glory may come in!" (Psalms 24:9)

Beyond Created Light

In April of 2016, a new episode of Star Wars came into the theaters; *"The Force Awakens."* Due to our extensive travel and other aspects of ministry, Tamera and I were unable to find the time to watch it. One mid-summer day, we both had a Stars Wars epiphany, *"Hey, Stars Wars is on its last week in the theaters, let's go see it before it leaves."* Without hesitation, we headed to a nearby theater to watch the latest galactic action of Star Wars.

Now there is one thing I need to tell you about Tamera, she is one of the most animated movie watchers you will probably ever experience in your lifetime. True story. ☺

Whenever I watch a movie with Tamera, it is our custom to set in the very back of the theater, so the rest of the audience is not held hostage by her intense response to the action of the movie.

I have no doubt; most people would probably pay a little extra to watch a movie with Tamera, since it would most likely give them the pleasure of experiencing a double feature.

I digress. We were sitting in the back of the theater, eager to take in the action. Given the fact the movie was on its last week of showing, there were not a whole lot of people in our section. ☺

During the course of the movie, there were a few times, when I had to hold on to Tamera, in fear of her completely ejecting out of her seat. In addition, while those around us were a safe distance away, I still felt it was necessary to take her invisible saber away.

Then the mega scene; when the Death Star was drawing energy from the sun in order to blow up a populated planet within its sphere.

It was at this moment, when I was suddenly arrested by the voice of the Lord.

He said,

"Do you know there is more energy and light in you than there is in the sun?" "What?" I shockingly replied. I thought, "How could that be?" The Lord continued, "What you are looking at is created light, but inside of you is creative light. The very light that spoke all things into being is in you. Therefore, there is more light and energy in you, than there is in the sun, moon, stars or any other created form of light." Wow!

The phrase "created light verses creative light" was really nothing new to me. I had come into this revelation a number of years ago. However, I was suddenly struck by an awesome reality of the functional capacity of the light of God in me, thus his people.

For years, I have spoken about our creative ability to not only predict the future, but to create it. To call upon things that are not yet visible, but seeing them by the spirit, thereby, making them visible. This is our creative potential in the kingdom of God. We are the destined guardians of both the natural and spiritual realm.

The light and energy of God in us is destined to create new frontiers that will reveal the heart and glory of God greater than any other generation before us.

We are not just the created ones, but we are the creative ones. Like our Father, we will say, **"Let there be light"** and there will be new forms of light, which will far exceed any other created/formed light.

Yes, I know, this is not for the faint hearted, nor is it for someone who has limited their eternal potential in the kingdom of God. We are born creators. This is why an innumerable field of created objects surrounds the world of humanity.

We were born to create. As great as all of this architecture is, it is merely baby steps toward our fullest creative potential in God. Our greatest creative moments will not just come from the hands of the flesh, but from the creative eternal realms of heaven in us.

One morning, Tamera and I were driving down the road in the Pacific Northwest. I said, "Let's engage with heaven. Let's walk upon a pathway, sense our surroundings, and see what happens."

By faith, we began to engage with heaven. While driving down the road, we started sharing with each other our encounters. Amazingly, we began to see much of the same things.

I can't remember how it all came about, but somehow the image of a painter appeared in our conversation. As this painter moved her brush across the canvas, everything she painted came alive. Suddenly, a beautiful bird with astounding color, landed on the shoulder of the painter.

47

Within a matter of seconds, this same bird flew right into the painting and continued its journey into another world. We both laughingly rejoiced over what had just happened.

I was reminded of the time when my friend John Filler had invited me to the home of Akiane Kramarik, who is one of the world's leading realistic painters. As I stared into these life like paintings, it was as though a gateway had opened up in the spirit, inviting me into another realm of the kingdom of God.

In the future, there will be an uncanny field of artistry, which will serve as eternal portals or gateways into the kingdom of God. It will redefine what creative paintings and writings are really all about. Just like the word of God, these insightful revelations will afford countless people the ability to engage with all creation in unimaginable ways.

Conduits Of Light

In December of 2015, in the spirit, I saw an image in the shape of a very long conduit. It was a piped conduit made of light. It had a fluid like substance flowing through it. It looked like it was about 5 inches or more in diameter. I knew it was a future technology that would serve as a type of conduit for the purpose of transferring substances from one place to another. It was undoubtedly some type of "formed light."

This is just one of many examples of future *"light technology"* and its many capabilities. Light as we understand it today is about to dramatically change. Seemingly, on a daily basis, new revelations concerning light are coming into view. I recently came across this article, written on *September 11, 2014 by Stephen Luntz.*

"Scientists Create Solid Light." *Princeton University, Engineering School, by creating a "self-trapping regime" scientist has made light behave like a crystal."*

The article goes on to say how science has discovered a way to lock individual photons together so they become like a solid object. Wow! Seriously?

Quantum physics states, *"as you go deeper and deeper into the workings of the atom, you see there is nothing there – just waves of energy."* It also describes an atom as an actual invisible force field, a kind of miniature tornado, which emits waves of electrical energy.

Those energy waves can be measured and their effects seen, but they are not a material reality, they have no substance because they are merely a form of electricity. Thus, most of the world of science embraces the idea that the universe is made of energy, or light.
Sound familiar? *"Let there be light..."* I found some articles on the Internet that revealed some amazing insight about our physical makeup. I discovered we are made up of atoms and atoms are continuously giving off and absorbing light and energy all the time.

This action of energy doesn't stop, even when we're sleeping. Every cell in the body has its atoms lined up in such a way that it has a negative and a positive voltage, inside and out. So every cell in our body is like a miniature battery. Each cell has 1.4 volts of energy. This doesn't sound like much, but when you multiply by the number of cells in your body (50 trillion) you get a total voltage of 70 trillion volts of electricity in your body.

Now that's a pretty strong current. This is what the Chinese refer to as **"chi."** Of course, as children of God, we know the ultimate source of healing comes via the energy of the Holy Spirit.

Today, through sophisticated instruments, we have the ability to measure this unusual force of energy in the human body. Science has proven the heart has the strongest electromagnetic energy field.

"Out of the heart flow the springs of life." (Proverbs 4:23) In addition, science has come to the conclusion there's no such thing as matter.

How amusing it is that fifty years ago Nietzsche declared that God is dead, and fifty years from now science will have to declare that God is alive and that matter is dead. ☺

As science goes deeper and deeper into the understanding of matter it finds that matter disappears and only energy remains.

In other words, we really are beings of light. In fact, at one level or another, all creation is made of light.

When science dug deep, it found only energy exists and when delved deeper you find that only spirit and soul exists.

Yes, even soul is energy. The time is just around the corner when a synthesis of science and spirit will be achieved, and the line between the two will simply disappear.

The gap between science and spiritual truth is quickly coming to a close, which means the gap between science and spirit will eventually vanish as well. These ancient lines of separation are destined to dissolve into the light of the maturation of the sons and daughters of God. If matter and consciousness are no longer two, how can spirit and science be two?

The separation of science and spirit has always been dependent on the separation of matter and spirit. Yes, it's true. We are on the edge of one of the greatest emergences the world has ever known.

One of which, I believe, will revolutionize the world in unimaginable ways.

Time Warp

Like a diamond, time is multifaceted, both in heaven and on Earth. On Earth, time serves as a type of guardian, until we become spiritually mature enough to break the barrier of time, thus removing its limitations on our life. Of course, from an earthly perspective, time is the instigator of human decay. Therefore, the objective is to come out from under the government of time, thus decay, putting it beneath our feet.

Time was designed to confine the enemy, not the sons and daughters of God. The moment sin came through the gateway of humanity; time became an expectant barrier to be broken, thus a guardian toward spiritual maturity.

Currently, Earth and all of its inhabitants are subject to time. In fact, everything in the natural realm is time sensitive. From sun up to sundown, we are seemingly working against the clock. The idea of "working against the clock" implies time is working against us rather than for us.

Time was meant to serve mankind, not the other way around.

Again, time is a force of government on Earth. Time does not exist in heaven in the same manner it does on Earth. In the eternal realms of God, the function of time is measured differently than on Earth.

The Psalmist David writes,

"For a thousand years in Your sight are like yesterday when it passes by, or as a watch in the night." (Psalms 90:4)

I find it interesting that many endtime theologians have used this passage of scripture as a rule of measurement for predicting the end of the world. David is not saying, in the eyes of God, 1000 years equal a day. He is simply pointing out that time on Earth does not function the same as it functions in heaven. Therefore, in terms of time, a thousand years is **like** a single day on Earth.

From a physiological perspective, time, space and light, in heaven, do not work or look anything like it does on Earth. Time, space and light on Earth, for the most part, operate in a reductive state.

A number of years ago, prior to speaking at a public meeting, I was seeking the Lord for understanding concerning some prior revelation he had shown me about his kingdom manifesting on the Earth.

During this prayer time, I saw a huge curtain being pulled back by some invisible hand. In the spirit, I leaned through the opening of this invisible curtain as if sticking my head through a giant window. When I did, I could see what looked like unusual creatures flying all around me. They were swooping down in front of my face. I couldn't make out all the details of their apparent glory, but I could clearly hear the sound of their voices and the intensity of their movement.

I soon realized they were flying around a giant figure standing in front of me. His feet were like iron and as I continued to gaze upward, his entire body looked as though it was made of various metals. From what I could make out, it looked like a giant robot. One of the first things that came to mind was the movie, "Transformers" even though this encounter was way before that time.

As my gaze reached the top, I could see its head shimmering in a golden light. It reminded me of some intense ancient warrior dressed for battle.

This experience reminded me of the dream Nebuchadnezzar had in Daniel's day.

It was as though I was being caught up into some kind of time warp. What seemed like a very long time, turned out to be less than an hour. Even though it was a short time on Earth, it was sufficient to make me late for my meeting.

After arriving to my destination I quickly approached the stage. When I did, I could see a visible cloud in front of me. This cloud had some of the makings of my experience I just had at home.

As I begin to speak, a tangible glory could be seen and felt by everyone in the meeting. Within a matter of minutes, practically everyone in the entire tent was laid out on the ground. It was as though the residue of my previous experience stayed with me and overflowed into the meeting. I distinctly remember having an unusual sense we were being caught up into some kind of spiritual time warp.

In the book of Revelation, John writes,

"When the Lamb broke the seventh seal, there was silence in heaven for about half an hour." (Revelation 8:1)

Since a day to God is like a thousand years, I think it's safe to say a half hour in heaven is not the same as it is on Earth. That single half hour could equate into multiple years.

In the kingdom of heaven, all that pertains to time operates in its original eternal state. Obviously, all that is in the kingdom realm of heaven functions outside of any earthly limitations. In heaven, light and glory are not in a reductive state. In heaven, light is not measured like it's measured on Earth. The laws of time on Earth do not exist in heaven. In heaven, time is perpetual, without interruption, without end.

In the kingdom of God, the light of God, in of itself is the government of God, because God is light. **Light is who God is not just what he has.** Light in heaven is perceptional, revelation, illumination, love, glory, etc. Most importantly, God is love, which is much different than saying, 'God has love.' God has everything and is everything. The light and love of God are the government of God.

"This is the message we have heard from him and declare to you: God is light; in him there is no darkness at all." (1John 1:5)

If light from the sun can accelerate growth on Earth at an amazing rate, how much more can the unapproachable light of God accelerate everlasting life?

One of the primary differences between eternal and everlasting life is the first has no beginning or end, while the second has a

56

beginning, without end. In heaven, the tenses of time: past, present and future, are readily accessible at any given moment. Outside the fullness of eternity, creation is governed by times and seasons. In the eternal abode of God, times and seasons exist, but do not govern heaven. All of which, are free of decay.

It is the supreme intent of God to bring his people into a sphere of spiritual maturity that will enable them to engage with the eternal side of creation at every level in the spirit of love. I must echo this again, in the interim; time is a spiritual guardian until we become spiritually mature enough to place it under our feet. Placing time under our feet is the same as placing death and decay under our feet.

I believe this final act of spiritual maturation will instigate the final return or appearing of Jesus, thus handing everything over to the Father.

"For as in Adam all die, so also in Christ all will be made alive. But each in his own order: Christ the first fruits, after that those who are Christ's at His coming, then comes the end, when He hands over the kingdom to the God and Father, when He has abolished all rule and all authority and power. For He must reign until He has put all His enemies under His feet. The last enemy that will be abolished is death." (1Cor 15:22-26)

Carriers Of Time

*"**Eternity is in our hearts.**"* Many think this is just a nice spiritual metaphor for eventually living a life without end. I believe it means we are literally carriers of time. We are **"time carriers."** Remember, the kingdom of heaven is in us. Therefore, inside of us, are all the cycles of times and seasons.

The moment humanity was restored in Christ, time, as we understand it, came into submission to the sons and daughters of God. Even though the fullness of that submission is not yet evident, as we continue on the road to spiritual maturity, our eternal habitation in the kingdom of God, and our authority over time, will become far more evident.

The Earth is currently the Lord's footstool, which means time is subjected to the rule of God.

*"**Heaven is my throne, And the Earth the footstool of my feet...**" (Acts 7:49)*

Since we are seated in heavenly places, this means time is destined to become our footstool as well. However, the majority of people are still inching their way into this kingdom revelation. Yet, even as I write this, countless men, women and children are breaking the barrier of time and space. They are moving about freely in the kingdom of heaven. They are supernaturally defying the laws of physics, matter and gravity. From an eternal perspective, all of these natural laws are an illusion.

In the early 2000's, I began to frequently encounter the cosmos. Yes, I know this statement sounds a bit ludicrous. Nonetheless, God showed me the outer limits of space and many of its hidden mysteries.

Most of these encounters occurred during times of corporate worship. The Lord would often take me beyond the visible realm of space into areas where various planets and other forms of creation had not yet been realized. At first, I thought it was just my imagination. Then I realized God was using my imagination as a type of gateway to give me access to the outer limits of space. Eventually, as technology advanced, it confirmed many of my own personal discoveries.

At this point, my understandings of creation began to increase. Prior to that time, I barely had a basic knowledge of astronomy, let alone specific knowledge of hidden mysteries in the galaxies.

Eventually, I ended up writing a book titled, *"Space The Prophetic Frontier."* This book is basically a diary of my initiation as a prophet and my wild encounters with the future and the cosmos. On the pathways of my prophetic journey, many wondered if I had literally lost my mind. Of course, I didn't blame them, because I had wondered the same thing.

Let me speed things up.

Science has already proven that **"mass"** is really non-existent. What was once believed to be mass is really particles of light, thus atoms, protons and molecules grouped together manifesting what we call *"formed matter."*

In short, matter really doesn't matter.

While many are still tampering with the basic realities of life, many others are advancing into their eternal inheritance; so much so, they are beginning to exhibit a generation that will never die, which brings me to my next perspective of time.

Length Of Years

In the late 80's, Kim Clement was one of the first prophets I ever heard speak about the future within the context of a couple hundred years. This glorious perspective of the future impacted me greatly.

In addition, Dr. Harold Eberle (Worldcast Ministries) wrote a book entitled, "Glorious Eschatology." This book greatly influenced my life as well. Since then, over the years, people have asked, "how much time do we have left?" My response, "More years than most can imagine."

Of course, this never set's well with those who are expecting the final curtain of judgment to be drawn at any moment.

The final chapter is not the end of all things, but the beginning of all things. All that is destined to come to an end is chaos, disunity and ultimately corruption's final demise.

Our expected lifespan on Earth is directly linked to the increasing appearing of Jesus Christ in his people, which will ultimately invite the restoration of all things. We were originally born out of the light of God's love, not out of darkness. Limitations and decay are a byproduct of darkness or obscured perception.

If we walk in the light as He is in the light, there will be no end as to what we can see or do.

"This is the message we have heard from him and proclaim to you, that God is light, and in him is no darkness at all. If we say we have fellowship with him while we walk in darkness, we lie and do not practice the truth. But if we walk in the light, as he is in the light, we have fellowship with one another, and the blood of Jesus his Son cleanses us from all sin." (1John 1:5-7)

I have come to realize the amount of time any one person has on Earth depends on their choices, purpose and relationship in God. However, I do not believe "length of years" on Earth was ever meant to be a goal in life.

No matter how long the length of our days on Earth, might be, it is but a brief moment compared to eternity. Having said that, I believe we are afforded the opportunity to walk in a measure of eternity now. As stated earlier, like Enoch, we have an invitation from heaven to walk in no decay now and then one day; step out of this realm into the fullness of heaven.

In the meantime, we are privilege to steward our time wisely. In light of eternity, I do not believe God ever intended longevity on Earth to become our primary pursuit. How many times have you heard the phrase, "you only live once?"

This perspective is completely void of an eternal revelation. From an eternal perspective, this life is just the beginning of an endless journey of love in the kingdom of God.

While length of days with family and friends is a valuable part of our Earthly journey; all are but a brief moment of the eternal intent of God to unite all of his sons and daughters in the bond of his everlasting love.

Prior to mankind's initial act of disobedience, time was never a part of the governmental equation, at least not in the manner it is today. Unlike today, time before sin was not a governing force to be reckoned with. This means age was never a factor. Although you might see someone in heaven who looks like they are 20, from an eternal perspective, they are neither young nor old. The fact we assess them according to how old they look proves we are still subject to the knowledge of good and evil.

Which leads me to this thought; from a Hebraic perspective "good and evil" is more accurately interpreted as function and dysfunction. When God said, *"Let there be light and saw that it was good,"* it literally meant, God saw it was functional. In other words, light was functioning according to its intended purpose.

In Eden, prior to sin, as far as mankind was concerned, function and dysfunction was not a factor. In their minds, one form of creation was not measured against another in terms of being less functional than the other.

In the beginning, God said,

"...From any tree of the garden you may eat freely, but from the tree of the knowledge of good (functional) and

evil (dysfunctional) you shall not eat, for in the day that you eat from it you will surely die." (Gen 2:16-17)

Contrary to popular belief, eating from the tree of knowledge of function and dysfunction was not about eating an apple or some other natural fruit, it was about tasting of a realm, which had the ability to lead mankind into a realm of dysfunction, which was contrary to the eternal design of God. Prior to sin, decay had no point of access into creation.

Once mankind tasted of this realm, they were seduced from a limitless to a limited state, thus the government of function and dysfunction.

Before sin, mankind viewed itself from an eternal perspective, not an earthly one. In this case, "opened eyes" represented a shift in government. The eventual visible/natural realm began to overlay the invisible/spiritual realm. Again prior to sin, man was not subject to the limiting laws of the physics of time.

The phrase **"in the day that you eat"** indicates if you taste of this realm (function and dysfunction) you will be subject to the government of function and dysfunction, which is time, thus decay will set in and you will surely die.

Prior to the initial act of disobedience, time was subservient to mankind, not the other way around. Thus, the platform for future constitutional governments was set into motion.

Constitutional Guardians

Like the Law, the Constitution of these United Sates, serves as a temporary guardian, until the intended government of heaven resumes its place in the heart of humanity.

In reference to the ministry of Moses, Paul writes,

But if the ministry of death, in letters engraved on stones, came with/in glory, so that the sons of Israel could not look intently at the face of Moses because of the glory of his face, fading as it was, how will the ministry of the Spirit fail to be even more with glory? For if the ministry of condemnation has/had glory, much more does the ministry of righteousness abound in glory. For indeed what had glory, in this case has no glory because of the glory that surpasses it. "For if that

which fades away was with/in glory, much more that which remains is in glory." (2Corinthians 3:7-11)

We can see the ministry of Moses, the Law, had glory, yet it does not have glory today. In its day, if the people stepped out of line, then the glory of Moses literally condemned them to death. It's incredibly sad how much of the spiritual leadership of this day still try to use an old glory, the Law, to manipulate people into a life of obedience.

It's nothing more than a desperate attempt to control the actions of people, hoping to persuade them into some form of religious submission.

As I mentioned at the beginning of this book, the Law, was a tutor or guardian to faith. Before the Law, sin was not imputed against mankind.

"For until the Law, sin was in the world, but sin is not imputed when there is no law." (Romans 5:13)

Though the action of sin was no less deadly, before the Law, there was no method to measure its severity.

Through the Law, a line was drawn in the sand. One of its primary purposes was to keep the people from self-destruction. Once Jesus appeared on the scene, the glory of the Law gave way to the glory of grace and faith. Through this transition a former glory gave way to a latter glory, an old covenant for a new covenant.

Like the law, the constitution of these United States is a guardian to spiritual maturity. The Constitution is an historical document that embodies the fundamental laws and principles by which the United States is governed. It was drafted by the Constitutional

Convention and later supplemented by the Bill of Rights and other amendments.

However, as great as these laws and principles are, they were never intended to become the final stage of government for these United States. At best, they were given as a guardian to spiritual maturity, at which time; the body of Christ will manifest its heavenly governing authority on the Earth.

Imagine if you will, all of the constitutional amendments that govern the United States, one day becoming a thing of the past because the government of heaven reigns on the Earth as it reigns in heaven.

On October 1, 2015 another tragic and senseless shooting took place on a college campus in Roseburg, Oregon. On the heels of this tragic event it didn't take long for the heads of government to make it about gun control. I have to say; I think both sides of this issue are missing the mark.

One side believes that the regulation of fewer guns will make a difference while the other side believes the regulation of more guns is the better alternative. It is believed that the reasons for these tragic events vary from mental health, gun control, inadequate security and just plain evil.

It's important to remember, at the end of the day, we are not wrestling against flesh and blood, but powers and principalities of the air. *(Eph. 6:12)*

While I do believe it is important to protect our second amendment rights (the right to bear arms) I also believe it's far more important to understand no matter how many guns you have in your possession, it will never be sufficient to counteract the works of the enemy.

Again, before I delve deeper into this subject, I want to emphasis the love of God is, and will always be, the greatest constitution for all of humanity. However, I do believe the second amendment, along with the rest of the constitution of the United States is a guardian to spiritual maturity.

The fact that anyone has to carry a gun to protect themselves is a clear indication that we have yet to enter into our greater supernatural inheritance in the kingdom of God.

Though Jesus, through his death and resurrection, disarmed all the power of the enemy, he is still waiting for us to access the kingdom realms of heaven and govern the Earth in the manner he has called us to, thus placing every evil work under our feet. Placing the enemy "under our feet" ultimately comes through the revelation of governing from heaven down, not Earth up.

Chris Mintz, while a student of Oregon's Umpqua Community College, was shot 7 times because he put himself between a shooter on campus and the rest of the students. His heroic actions proved to be a very selfless act, which in my opinion demonstrates true heroism.

Nonetheless, the question should be asked, what would be the expectant response of the sons/daughters of God who understand their authority in the kingdom of heaven? I think it would sound and look something like this;

"You spirit of death, I bind you in the name of Jesus and declare you will not exercise your evil intent in this place!"

As men and women of God, this type of response will be a normal reaction toward any unwanted circumstance of the enemy.

As children of God, through the spirit of love, we are being invited to exercise our kingdom authority of heaven on Earth. You might be thinking this is just for the selected few, the most gifted or anointed, but this is for anyone knows who they are in the kingdom of God.

Let me share a brief experience with you.

A number of years ago, I was conducting an outdoor tent meeting in Yakima, WA. It was during a time when a lot of new gangs were walking the streets looking for potential members. This recruiting process always required some type of initiation to prove a new members loyalty to the gang.

During one of our evening meetings, a tall native man approached me at the front of the tent while I was speaking to the people. He walked right up to me, nose to nose, and spit in my face. Everyone watching seem to be frozen in their seats.

I noticed a small green military looking bag hanging off of his right shoulder. Little did I realize in the bag was a long army bayonet. We discovered later the tip of the knife was sticking out of the bag about 2-3 inches.

The objective was to ram the knife into my stomach, thus being promoted to a higher position in the gang. For whatever reason, without hesitation, I grabbed the face of the man in front of me with both hands and pulled his face into mine. I then said, "In the name of Jesus, you murdering spirit I command you to come out of this man now!"

I suddenly heard a rumbling noise coming out of his stomach. He then slumped to the ground, but not before trying to bite my neck like some hungry vampire.

The Lord spoke to me, "Michael, I want to move now!" I loudly repeated what I heard. "The Lord wants to move now!" It was as if a misty cloud appeared in the tent. Observers from the outside, some of which were part of the gang initiation, came running into the tent toward the front.

At first I thought, "Oh man, this doesn't look good." As they got just a few feet away from me, they threw their hands up in the air and fell backwards. It was as though they ran into some invisible wall.

Later on, after thinking about everything that had happened, I came to the realization they encountered a very large angel. One thing for sure, they were knocked out cold by the power of God. Sometime later, after they awoke, they were clearly overwhelmed with the love and power of God.

Before the night was over, everyone in and around the tent was supernaturally impacted by the power of God. Needless to say, it was truly a divine interruption. What the enemy intended for evil, God turned for the good.

On a much larger scale, in order for me to convince you further as to why I believe the military might of this nation or any other nation is merely a guardian destined to give way to the supernatural authority of heaven on Earth, I need to draw your attention to an experience the prophet Elisha had with an entire Syrian military force.

In *2 Kings 6*, the king of Syria was constantly trying to make a surprise attack against Israel. However, every time the king worked out what seemed to be a perfect plan, Israel would become aware of the king's plans and change their route. At first, the

Syrian king thought someone in his own army was forewarning Israel of his plans.

When the king demanded to know who was betraying him, it was brought to his attention the prophet Elisha supernaturally was gaining knowledge of the king's plans, thus warning Israel of his intent. As soon as the king realized what was going on, he sent an entire army to take out Elisha.

The rest of the story is a picture of the Syrian army closing in on Elisha and his servant. The important thing that set Elisha apart from anyone else who might find themselves in a similar situation; Elisha could see the invisible army of God was with him. In the natural, there were only two people, Elisha and his servant, against an army of hundreds, possibly thousands. However, in the spirit it was no contest.

Also, this chapter notes Elisha asking God to open the eyes of the servant so he could see the massive army of God in the spirit. This spiritual dimension consisted of angels, horses and fiery chariots. This same army was ready to move against the enemy on Elisha's behalf. There is a very important thing to note here. As great as the army of God was, this massive angelic force did not actually have to engage with the Aramean army.

In **2 King 6:18-19** reads,

"When they came down to him, Elisha prayed to the LORD and said, "Strike this people with blindness, I pray." So He struck them with blindness according to the word of Elisha. Then Elisha said to them, "This is not the way, nor is this the city; follow me and I will bring you to the man whom you seek." And he brought them to Samaria."

What was the deal with the angelic force? Were they just a backup in case things got out of hand? I believe it was a declaration to Elisha and his servant, 'you are not alone.' Those who are with you are more than those who are against you. Seeing beyond the natural realm afforded Elisha the courage and boldness to walk in the authority given to him by God. In addition, the servant was afforded the same opportunity to step out of fear into the reality of heaven on Earth. In a sense, we could say the revelation of the army of God was a guardian to spiritual maturity for Elisha and his servant. God used one man to not only stand against an entire army, but to lead them into captivity.

When the Aramean army was blinded, they were blinded to who Elisha was and their current location. When they began to advance they thought they were in one place when in fact they were in another. It wasn't until they came to Samaria their eyes were opened and they discovered they were standing in the enemy's camp.

They were literally relocated from one city to the next and didn't even know it. Through one bold and courageous man, God overcame an entire army. This is but one of many examples in scripture of how God demonstrates the power he has invested in his people.

All of the above depicts a glorious government given to those who can see beyond the natural realm into the kingdom of heaven. The time is now at hand, when we will see men and women of God breaking free from an earthly constitution, thus exhibiting a heavenly one.

The guardians of the constitution of the United States have postured themselves; making way for a supernatural government, which will super exceed every earthly form of government.

A time is soon coming when the people of God will stand on modern day battlefields and supernaturally disarm armies of destruction. In addition, they will exemplify the love of God, thus revealing the constitution of heaven on Earth.

Whether they are in schools, businesses, places of entertainment, or any other kingdom in the world, all will be subjected to the constitution of the love of God. While these words might seem impossible now, soon, many will depart from an old limited government into an unlimited constitution of heavenly glory.

Guardians Of Health

I am so grateful we have the medical minds of today working diligently in the fields of medicine and science.

Their quest for great success is certainly commendable. Even in the realm of natural medicine, its impact toward humanity has gone off the charts of previous understanding.

There seems to be no end to the increasing knowledge of healthcare sweeping across the world.

Though there are areas in the world still trying to catch up with some of the basic necessities of healthcare. I am convinced a time is soon coming when every nation in the world will be afforded the opportunity to effectively live free from most diseases.

In addition, as a world society, we are crossing over the threshold where physical hunger will eventually become a thing of the pass. This is not to say there will not be the continual challenge of a poverty mentality. Nonetheless, the increasing supernatural transformation of hearts and minds will surpass any other generation before us.

Nonetheless, as great as the expertise of medical science may be, at best, it's still a mere guardian to spiritual maturity. We are so privileged to be living in a time when the knowledge of all things, both natural and spirit, are continually being redefined. We are beginning to see clear evidence of a spiritual maturity emerging to such extent; the supernatural authority of heaven on Earth is being displayed in unimaginable ways.

Historically, we can see the progression of God's kingdom increasing on the Earth. The baton of Kingdom advancement is repeatedly being handed off from one generation to the next. Now we have come to another historical handoff. The transference of revelatory glory is revealing the ancient pathways of heaven on Earth.

A time is soon coming when atmospheres within cities and regions will be saturated with the glory of God, so intensely, countless people will be impacted by the revelation knowledge of God's love.

The intensity of this glory will become the gateway to bringing sickness and disease under the authority of God's people.
In conjunction with this amazing love-fest of glory invading the Earth, the entire medical industry is, and will be, greatly influenced by newfound technologies that will surpass any previous medical understanding.

A recent article published in **"Men's Health Magazine"** describes a new technology that unveils the design of a bionic eye.

"The "Argus II" takes a video signal from a camera built into sunglasses and wirelessly transmits that image to implants in the retinas of people who have lost their vision.

Though it's been available in Europe since 2011, the U.S. Food and Drug Administration (FDA) only approved the eye earlier this year."

"This really is Star Trek technology, Dr. Roizen says."

I remember in the early 70's when a television series titled "The Six Million Dollar Man" became a big hit.

The Six Million Dollar Man was a science fiction and action series about a former astronaut, Colonel Steve Austin, portrayed by American actor Lee Majors.

Austin ended up with superhuman strength due to bionic implants and became employed as a secret agent by a fictional U.S. government office, named OSI. To say the least, as a young man, for me it seemed like a very hopeful possibility for the future.

Now, fast forward, here we are in the future and the possibility of a working bionic eye is indeed a current reality. Not to mention all the other bionic inventions on the market today.

Another amazing medical science breakthrough is in the area of the brain, specifically in the area of seizures.

"For the 840,000 epileptics suffering from sudden, uncontrollable seizures, the NeuroPace is like "a defibrillator for your brain," Dr. Roizen says."

Dr. Roizen writes, *"This system includes sensors implanted in the brain that can spot the first tremors of an oncoming seizure. Then it sends electrical pulses that counteract the brain's own haywire signals, stopping the seizure in its tracks."*

This is without a doubt a very big deal. The bible says, *"Every good thing comes from above."* Yet, at the end of the day, as great as these amazing discoveries are, at best, they are mere guardians toward spiritual maturity, hence supernatural health. They are given to us until we enter into the fullness of the power of God, thus exhibiting our intended supernatural reign in the kingdom of our Father. In the meantime, we gratefully celebrate all of these amazing breakthroughs that are affording humanity a greater quality of life. However, in the end, this road toward divine health is yet another guardian toward no decay. More clearly known as "immortality."

Guardians Of The Elements

My purpose for bringing this topic to light is to enforce the fact; as sons and daughters of God, we are destined to take authority over all the elements of creation. All of which are in a decayed state. When sin entered into the world, the spirit of decay affected all creation.

However, since the resurrection of Jesus, we have been reinstated into our original state in the kingdom of God, thus an ongoing restoration of all things. This restorative power includes all the elements, as in the elements of the periodic table, which are on the brink of being redefined. I use the term "redefined" because these elements are destined to be restored to their original state.

Now don't get nervous when I use the word "alchemy." In order to convey your supernatural ability over every element in the universe, I need to challenge some of our understanding about the periodic table. I have spent a little time looking into the history of the ancient practice of alchemy, which is becoming more of a frequent subject, even in the Christian community.

What was once considered to be an occulted practice is now proving to be nothing less than an extended knowledge from heaven. While many view this type of practice in a negative light, let me share some biblical insight concerning alchemy.

What is Alchemy?

Before the sixth and seventh centuries after Christ, a large percentage of scientific practices were later called, "alchemy." During these same periods, alchemy was widely known as "the Sacred Arts, Occult Science, Art of Hermes, or otherwise known as Hermetic Art." The word "alchemia" or "chemia", is where the word "chemistry" comes from. In the world of science, it is historically noted in the writings of Kopp that "chemia" (chemistry) was used to designate the art of metalworking. Then it was later believed, that you could change base metals into gold and silver.

In the Encyclopedia of Diderot, Paul-Jacques Malouin defines Alchemy as, *"an ancient tradition whose practitioners have claimed to be the precursor to profound ability and powers. It is the chemistry of the cleverest, which allows one to observe amazing chemical operations at a more rapid pace, operations that would normally require a long time for nature to produce."*

Historically, Malouin's definition of alchemy varies, but typically includes one or more of the following:

1) *The creation of the philosopher's stone. (a substance believed to change any metal into gold or silver)*

79

2) *The ability to transmute base metals into noble metals such as gold or silver.*

3) *The development of a life that would confer youth and longevity.*

Malouin goes on to write,

"Alchemy played a significant role in the development of early modern science, it is now recognized as proto-science that contributed to the development of modern chemistry and medicine."

Alchemists developed a structure of basic laboratory techniques, theory, terminology, and experimental method, some of which are still in use today. However, alchemists predated modern foundations of chemistry, such as scientific skepticism, atomic theory, the modern understanding of a chemical element and a chemical substance, the periodic table and conservation of mass and stoichiometry. Instead, they believed in four elements, and cryptic symbolism and mysticism was an integral part of alchemical work."

In previous articles/videos, I've shared prophetic insight the Lord gave to me regarding the "Periodic Table of Elements." There are approximately 118 elements listed, a few of which have been added because of chemical manipulation.

I believe the Lord has repeatedly told me, *"The periodic table would be redefined."*

Over the last number of years, by the spirit, I have seen minerals/elements in the ground and in the heavens above that have yet to be discovered. Over the last few years, all over the

80

world, the appearing of gemstones have become an increasing supernatural phenomena in the church.

This particular sign and wonder is part of a major upset in the current periodic table. Primarily, because gemologists say the substance of these stones cannot be identified. In addition, in the future, the current chart of elements will began to change simply because of the supernatural alteration of various metals of lesser value being converted into metals of much greater value, some of which, we have no record.

I believe one of the primary objects of Father is to bring us into a deeper revelation of his love. And, as odd as it may sound, having his sons and daughters exhibit authority over the elements of creation is part of the love walk of heaven on Earth. I believe every father should want their child to know their fullest and greatest potential. Such is the nature of our heavenly Father.

Recently, a good friend of mine sent me a recent article from *"ScienceNews."*

It reads:

"Researches at the University of California, created a super-strong yet light structural metal with extremely high specific strength and modulus, or stiffness-to-weight ratio. To create the super-strong but lightweight metal, the team, found a new way to disperse and stabilize nanoparticles in molten metals." (Science News December 23, 2015)

Another recent news report became a fulfillment of the previous prophetic word mentioned at the beginning of this chapter.

"Periodic table's seventh row finally filled as four new elements are added." This was the word the Lord gave to me, *"The periodic table will be redefined."*

The article goes on to say,

"Discovery of four super-heavy chemical elements by scientists in Russia, America and Japan has been verified by experts and formally added to the periodic table." (January 3, 2016. (Theguardian.com)

This is just a few of the amazing breakthroughs coming about in the world of science, which in the end will redefine many of the known medals today. Yet, this is merely a small road sign pointing toward the supernatural display of God's people exercising their authority over the basic elements of life.

In this sense, the current periodic table can be viewed as a guardian to spiritual maturity.

As stated earlier, the current periodic table is a decayed form of an eternal table that exists in heaven. There are amazing elements in the kingdom of heaven, which far exceed anything most have ever seen or imagined.

We are about to witness the appearing of the eternal table of elements on Earth as in heaven.

In the final stages of this supernatural creative transformative process, base metals and other seemingly concrete forms, will be supernaturally altered.

This kingdom authority will soon become common practice among the children of God.

The Bible gives testimony of this, not only in Old Testament scripture, but also in New Testament scripture.

In the Old Testament, the Bible speaks about a
borrowed an axe from his master. In the midst of h
head fell off into a nearby brook and was lost.

The servant went to Elisha and explained his dilemm
servant showed Elisha where the iron axe had sunk, El.
off a branch and threw it into the water. The Bible then describes
the branch swimming toward the axe head, at which time the axe
floated to the surface and connected itself to the branch.

In order for the axe head to float to the top there had to be some
form of transformation, either in the chemistry of the iron, or
within the physical laws of gravitation. **(2 Kings 6:1-7)**

This brings me to my next point of perceived mineral
transformation.

Transforming Matter

There are elements or substances in food, otherwise known as minerals. Minerals are essential to our daily diet. These minerals consist of calcium, phosphorus, magnesium, iron, iodine, selenium, sodium and zinc just to name a few. In earlier biblical history, Elisha was one of the few on record who exercised the ability to transform the basic minerals of life. And, as you will see, there were others who literally exhibited the ability to transform matter.

In *2Kings 4:38-44* we read,

"When Elisha returned to Gilgal, there was a famine in the land. As the sons of the prophets were sitting before him, he said to his servant, "Put on the large pot and

boil stew for the sons of the prophets." Then one went out into the field to gather herbs, and found a wild vine and gathered from it his lap full of wild gourds, and came and sliced them into the pot of stew, for they did not know what they were.

So they poured it out for the men to eat. And as they were eating of the stew, they cried out and said, "O man of God, there is death in the pot." And they were unable to eat. But he said, "Now bring meal (flour)." "He threw it into the pot and said, "Pour it out for the people that they may eat."

Then there was no harm in the pot. Now a man came from Baal-shalishah, and brought the man of God bread of the first fruits, twenty loaves of barley and fresh ears of grain in his sack. And he said, "Give them to the people that they may eat." His attendant said, "What, will I set this before a hundred men?" But he said, "Give them to the people that they may eat, for thus says the LORD, 'They shall eat and have some left over.' "So he set it before them, and they ate and had some left over, according to the word of the LORD."

In short, the servant apparently picked some bad berries, which were added to the pot of stew. It didn't take long before the prophets at the table became deathly sick. As soon as this became evident, Elisha told the servant to add meal into the poisonous pot.

Many have thought that the added meal, in of itself canceled out the poison. However, I believe the meal, that was added to the stew was part of a supernatural process that transformed a poisonous pot of stew into a nutritional meal Not only was the stew transformed into a great meal, but it also became an antidote of wellness for those who were already sick.

Many believe the chemical state of the meal was miraculously altered. In addition, this same meal was supernaturally multiplied to feed a hundred men. All of these actions are the result of the alteration of physics and chemistry. God performed a similar act through Moses when he changed water into blood. **(Exodus 7:14-19)**

Again, something had to happen to the chemistry of the water, thus changing its composition into another substance. And, what about the staff of Moses? When Aaron threw it on the floor of Pharaoh's court it was transformed into a serpent. The original Hebrew actually describes the serpent as a dragon. Just saying.

The first recorded miracle was when Jesus changed water into wine. Not just any wine, but the finest wine. **(John 2:1-10)**

In another instance, when the enemy was tempting Jesus in the desert, he said, *"If you are truly the Son of God then turn these rocks into bread."* Though Jesus refused, it's obvious the enemy knew Jesus had the power to alter the composition of rocks, in this case, turning them into bread.

Another supernatural change of physics was when Jesus walked on water. This could have been a matter of Jesus simply being elevated above a stormy sea.

Or, it could have been the composition of water blinking in and out of existence from one frequency to another. Not to mention, the raging climate around him, which had no affect on his body, which means, he somehow shifted to a different frequency.

And what about the famous *"mountain of transfiguration"* where the physical body of Jesus was literally transposed into light, at which time, Moses and Elijah appeared with Jesus.

Jesus was without a doubt, the ultimate alchemist of heaven on Earth. Every level of creation was subject to the authority of heaven in him, thus exposed to being altered from one state to another. Of course, the intensity of transformation was equally realized when mankind was changed from it's natural state of dust and converted into a new glorious creation, thus placing all things under our feet.

Though all of these things seem outrageous, they are but a small glimpse of the present hour we are living in. While many will continue to alter this economy with future innovations, countless others will create an economy through the transformational ability to alter the laws of physics.

Whether it be solids or liquids or simply the power of multiplication, (fishes and loaves) all the above and more are just the beginning of an unstoppable revelation of heaven on Earth.

Guardians Of The Five-Fold

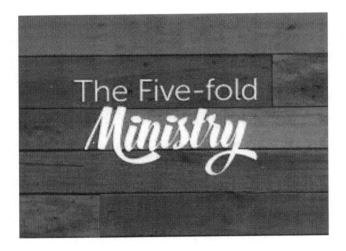

Lastly, I would like to shift into what the Ekklesia (church) terms the "five-fold." For the sake of time, I'm not going to take you down the repetitive road of kingdom function within the Church. Though I realize this five-fold governmental function is still not fully accepted by various religious systems, I still want to speak about this kingdom government as it pertains to all the kingdoms of the world.

While it is not my goal to devalue this amazing kingdom government given to the body of Christ, I would like to point out the importance of this heavenly government functioning in every kingdom, not just the kingdom of the church. I have long maintained my stance the governmental operation of the five-fold function serves as a constant reminder of the immaturity of the body of Christ.

One of the obvious signs of spiritual maturity is becoming less dependent on the training of spiritual leaders and more personally engaged with Father face to face, thus the eternal government of heaven.

I'm not saying we don't need each other, but our need for kingdom relationship was never meant to be a replacement for personal spiritual maturity. Again, true growth comes from walking in the love of God.

Paul writes,

"For though by this time you ought to be teachers, you have need again for someone to teach you the elementary principles of the oracles of God, and you have come to need milk and not solid food." (Hebrews 5:12)

In 2008, I wrote a book entitled, *"Evolution Of Another Kind."* In one of the chapters, I addressed the evolutionary process of the 5-fold ministry in the church. I termed this government as a spiritual force designed to cultivate **"a til generation."**

This understanding was inspired through a spiritual experience I encountered in 2006, which caused me to view **Ephesians 4** much differently than previous understanding.

"And He gave some as apostles, and some as prophets, and some as evangelists, and some as pastors and teachers, for the equipping of the saints for the work of service, to the building up of the body of Christ; until we all attain to the unity of the faith, and of the knowledge of the Son of God, to a mature man, to the measure of the stature which belongs to the fullness of Christ.

As a result, we are no longer to be children, tossed here and there by waves and carried about by every wind of doctrine, by the trickery of men, by craftiness in deceitful scheming; but speaking the truth in love, we are to grow up in all aspects into Him who is the head, even Christ, from whom the whole body, being fitted and held together by what every joint supplies, according to the proper working of each individual part, causes the growth of the body for the building up of itself in love. (Ephesians 4:11-16)

A "til" generation is referenced in verse 13,

"...until we all attain to the unity of the faith, and of the knowledge of the Son of God, to a mature man, to the measure of the stature which belongs to the fullness of Christ." (Ephesians 4:13)

I believe the maturation of the body of Christ is more evident today than any other time in history. Though we have a ways to go, we are nonetheless exemplifying the heart and mind of God increasingly every day.

This means, the visible evidence of a *"til generation"* is present now, revealing the kingdom of God upon the Earth in profound ways.

In light of this spiritual maturation, the five-fold government within the church and world is taking on an entire new look.

Again, the five-fold government working within the church was given for the equipping of the saints. Eventually there must come a time when the body of Christ reaches a level of maturation where the equipping process turns the corner into a greater revelation of the heart and mind of God inhabiting his people.

There is a difference between governing the church and equipping the church.

Unfortunately, there are many Christian leaders who have settled into the comfort of ruling over people, all in the name of spiritual maturity. It's a type of ownership mentality that wants to hang on to the people for the purpose of building their ministry.

Instead, they should be encouraging the people to leave the nest to engage with God and produce the kingdom of God in the manner to which they are called. When people are empowered to reach their full potential, they will assume the role of becoming more responsible; not only for their own lives, but also for helping others do the same.

Again, I do not believe, the government of God within the church, and the world, was ever meant to become the all in all, at least not in the sense of governing over people. The original design of heaven was to rule over creation, not humanity. Ruling over people is the result of sin entering the world.

"God created man in His own image, in the image of God He created him; male and female He created them. God blessed them; and said to them, "Be fruitful and multiply, and fill the Earth, and subdue it; and rule over the fish of the sea over the birds of the sky and over living thing that moves on the Earth." (Genesis 1:27-28)

Being reduced to governing over your own kind is nothing less than primitive government. In the end, we are lured into the illusion of wanting to rule over sons and daughters of God.

At best, the current visible government working in the church today is merely a guardian to spiritual maturity, at which time the evolution of God's kingdom in his people will become a supernatural revelation of his love, so much so, the entire world will recognize the body of Christ because of their love for one another.

In terms of spiritual maturation, there are countless treasures in heaven that are waiting to be accessed by the sons of God. These treasures were allotted to us, before time. When sin entered into the world, the pathways to the treasures of God eventually became less visible. All the pathways of God are connected to the kingdom of God and the kingdom of heaven, which are in us.

As our relationship with the Father develops, we are brought into a deeper more intimate awareness of the love of Jesus. Thus, the awareness of the riches of heaven and all that it affords us is clearly seen.

As I stated before, as long as the five-fold government operates within the church in the manner it does today, in terms of a hierarchal government, it will continually serve as a reminder of the immaturity of the body of Christ.

I am not implying the five-fold function is not a needed thing, but I do believe it's nearing the hour of a major alteration, at which time it will not look like anything we have ever seen before.
To say the least, this five-fold government is truly a guardian to spiritual maturity.

Obviously, this governmental operation in the kingdom of God has yet to reach its full maturation. Like stages of a rocket, as the body of Christ gains altitude it will disengage immaturity one stage at a time; taking on an entire new look and sound, thus exhibiting the intended order of heaven on Earth.

About The Author

Michael Danforth is the founder of Mountain Top International, which was established in 1998. He is also the founder of SOHL (School Of Higher Learning) and Kingdom Kreators. He is the author of several books. In addition, Michael is a musician and prophetic psalmist. He is internationally known for his gift of knowledge revelatory teaching and prophetic accuracy concerning personal prophecy and world events.

Michael and his wife Tamera, currently reside in Yakima, WA.

Mountain Top International

*****

Kingdom Kreators

PO Box 43 Yakima, WA 98907
www.mticenter.com

Evolution
of
Another
Kind

The Influence of Heaven on Earth

By Michael A. Danforth

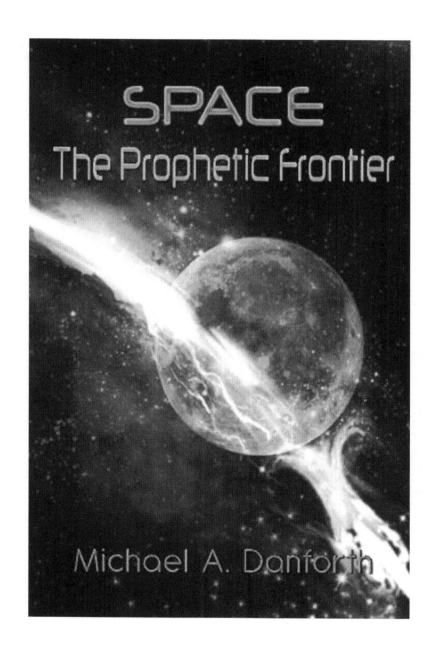

SPACE
The Prophetic Frontier

Michael A. Danforth

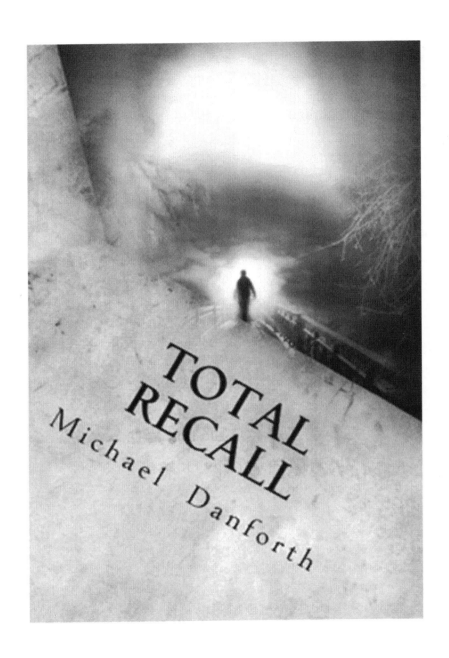

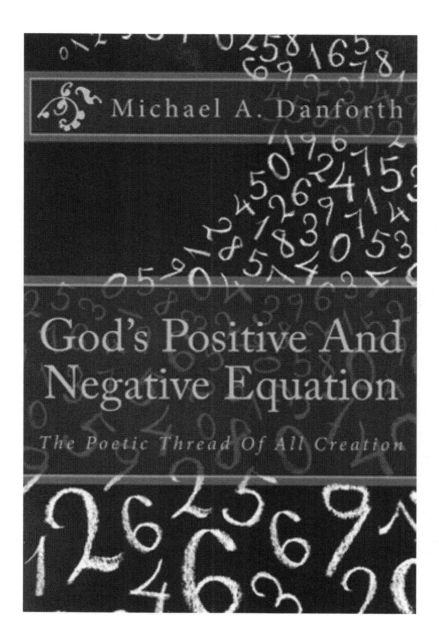

Michael A. Danforth

God's Positive And Negative Equation

The Poetic Thread Of All Creation

65502112R00057

Made in the USA
Lexington, KY
14 July 2017